GW01319713

Celebrations

JEWISH FESTIVALS

Jane Cooper

Wayland

Celebrations

Christmas
Easter
Hallowe'en
Harvest

Hindu Festivals
Jewish Festivals
Muslim Festivals
New Year

All words that appear in **bold** are explained in the glossary on page 46

First published in 1989 by
Wayland (Publishers) Limited
61 Western Road, Hove
East Sussex BN3 1JD, England

© Copyright 1989 Wayland (Publishers) Limited

British Library Cataloguing in Publication Data
Cooper, Jane
  Jewish festivals.
  1. Jewish festivals
  I. Title   II. Series
  296.4'3

ISBN 1 85210 822 3

Phototypeset by Kalligraphics Limited, Horley, Surrey
Printed and bound in Italy by G. Canale & C.S.p.A., Turin

Contents

Passover	4
The Feast of Weeks	14
The Feast of Tabernacles	18
The Festival of Lights	22
The Feast of Lots	26
The Jewish New Year	30
New Year for trees	36
Israel's Independence Day	38
Jerusalem Day	40
The Sabbath	42
The Jewish calendar	44
The Hebrew alphabet	45
Glossary	46
Books to read	47
Index	48

Passover

Passover is one of the most important festivals in the Jewish religion. It lasts for eight days and is held in March or April.

This picture of Passover celebrations was painted about 500 years ago.

The Passover story remembers an event which happened more than 3,000 years ago. At that time the Jewish people, known as the **Israelites**, lived in Egypt. For many years they were kept as slaves by the **Pharaohs**, or kings, of Egypt.

Passover celebrates the time the Jews left Egypt and were freed from slavery. This family is having a special meal to celebrate the beginning of Passover.

The Passover story tells how God told **Moses** to lead the Jews to freedom. At first the Pharaoh did not want to free the Jews. So God sent **plagues** to make the Egyptians suffer. He killed their children, but he 'passed over' the Jews and did not harm them. This is why the festival is called Passover. At last the Pharaoh begged Moses to take his people out of Egypt. This picture shows him pleading with Moses.

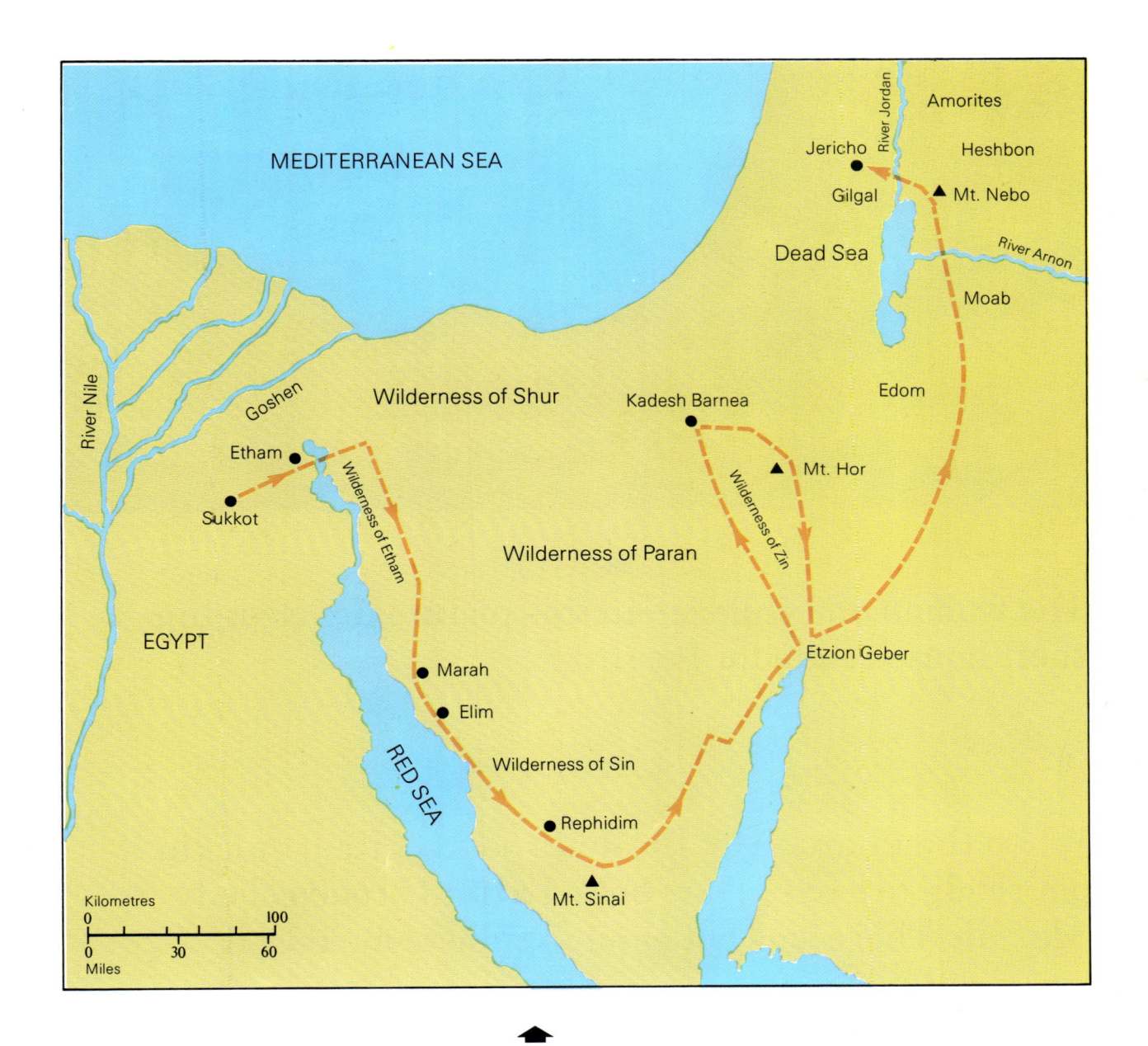

This map shows the route Moses and the Jews took when they left Egypt. The journey out of Egypt is called the **Exodus**.

The women and children in this picture are cleaning their house ready for Passover.

When the Pharaoh let the Jews go free, they quickly got ready to leave. They baked a hard bread called *Matzah*. There was not enough time to make soft bread with yeast.

Jewish families remember these events by cleaning their houses from top to bottom before Passover. They make sure there is no **leavened** food in the house, such as bread with yeast in it.

The first night of Passover is called Seder night. Families gather for the Seder meal. A plate of special foods is put in front of the father of the family.

There is *Matzah* bread and bitter herbs to remind Jews of the suffering in Egypt. Lettuce reminds them of spring. Cups of wine remind them of freedom. There is also a mixture of fruit and wine called *Charoset*, which looks like cement. This reminds people of the bricks used by the Jews when they were slaves and built the cities of Egypt.

◀ All the food and drink on the Seder table reminds people of the Jews' escape from Egypt.

The Passover festival is not just about the past. It also makes people think about the importance of freedom today and in the future.

◀ This stained glass window shows the Seder table with its special foods.

During the Seder ceremony, everyone has a copy of a book called the *Haggadah*. This tells the story of the Jews' escape from Egypt.

Recipes

Here are two Passover recipes. You could try to make your own *Charoset* or fried *Matzah*.

ASK AN ADULT TO HELP YOU BEFORE YOU START COOKING

To make *Charoset* you will need:
240g apples
60g raisins
60g almonds or walnuts
a sprinkle of cinnamon
a small amount of sweet wine

1 Peel and core the apples.
2 Chop them with the nuts and raisins.
3 Add cinnamon and mix with enough wine to make a paste.

To make fried *Matzah* you will need:
1 packet of *Matzah*
2 eggs, beaten together
vegetable fat or oil
0.25 litre milk
sugar, cinnamon, grated lemon rind

Break the *Matzah* into quarters and soak them in milk. Let them get soft but not soggy. Drain the *Matzah* and dip both sides in beaten egg.

Heat the fat or oil in a frying pan and fry both sides of the *Matzah* until they are light brown.

Serve sprinkled with sugar, cinnamon and grated lemon rind.

The Feast of Weeks

This festival takes place seven weeks after Passover. It is also called Pentecost.

The Feast of Weeks is when Jews remember part of the story of Moses. When the Jews left Egypt, they travelled into the **wilderness**. While they were in the wilderness Moses went up on to Mount Sinai. There, God gave him the **Commandments**. These are the laws and rules which Jews try hard to follow.

This painting shows Moses holding the stone tablets on which the Commandments were written. These Commandments became known as the *Torah*, or the Five Books of Moses.

The Feast of Weeks lasts two days. During this time, people remember the *Torah* being given to Moses.

The feast is also a summer harvest festival, held when the wheat is ripe. **Synagogues** are decorated with flowers and green leaves. These children are celebrating in **Israel**.

Jewish religious teachers are called **Rabbis**. This Rabbi is standing in a synagogue, in front of the Holy Ark. Each synagogue has a Holy Ark. This is the place where the Jewish holy book, the *Torah*, is kept. The *Torah* is written on **scrolls**.

Here you can have a closer look at some *Torah* scrolls. These were written by hand about 200 years ago. They are kept safe inside a decorated case. Each scroll is a holy object, and is looked after very carefully.

The word *Torah* does not have an exact English meaning. The nearest word is 'teaching'. The *Torah* contains all the rules and laws which tell Jews the right way to live. Over the years, many Rabbis have discussed the words of the Torah. All their thoughts are written in another set of holy books, which is called the *Talmud*.

It is more than 3,000 years since Moses received the Commandments. Followers of the Jewish religion are still guided by these laws today.

The Feast of Tabernacles

The Feast of Tabernacles is also called *Succot*. It reminds people that when the Jews escaped from Egypt, they wandered for forty years in the wilderness. During this time they sometimes lived in huts. Many people build a hut, called a *Succah*, in their home for the festival.

◀ This man is building a *Succah* in his garden.

In Israel, *Succot* celebrations are very colourful.

Succot lasts one week. During this time, meals may be eaten in the *Succah*. Some people even sleep there at night.

Succot is also a harvest festival. Branches of trees are used as decorations during ceremonies. They remind people of the harvest.

Long ago, there was a building in **Jerusalem** called the Holy Temple. It was built 2,500 years ago but later destroyed. Today, only the Western Wall of the Temple is still standing.

A very special ceremony was held at the Temple during *Succot*. Priests led a procession out of the Temple to a water well outside the city walls. There was music and singing.

This is a model of the Temple.
▼

Today, Jewish people remember these events at the time of *Succot*. Special food and drink is taken inside the *Succah*. People sing songs from the Bible and the Prayer Book.

The last day of the festival is called 'The Rejoicing of the Law'. On this day the *Torah* scrolls are carried seven times around the synagogue. Children join in the procession, and there is singing and dancing. These boys are joining in a procession.

The Festival of Lights

The Festival of Lights is called *Chanukah* in **Hebrew**. The festival lasts for eight days. A special candlestick, called a *Chanukiyah* is used. It can hold eight candles.

Every night of *Chanukah* an extra candle is lit. On the first night, one candle is lit. On the second night, two candles are lit. This goes on until the last night, when all eight candles are lit.

During *Chanukah* people remember another part of Jewish history.

About 2,000 years ago, the King of Syria tried to stop the Jews practising their religion. He sent an army which attacked the Jews and damaged their Temple at Jerusalem. The Jews fought against the Syrians, and in the end they defeated them. But when the Jewish soldiers cleaned the Temple, they found only one small lamp with oil in it. Lamps like these were needed to light the Temple candles.

Then a **miracle** happened. One little lamp of oil would normally burn for only a day. But the lamp the soldiers found went on burning for eight days.

This is a *Chanukah* service in a synagogue.

This old picture shows the Jews attacking the Syrian army.

The hero of the *Chanukah* story was a Jewish priest called Mattathias. He decided to fight against the King of Syria so that the Jews could remain free.

Mattathias and his five sons began a war against the Syrians. The war lasted for some years. In the end the Jews defeated the Syrians.

This giant *Chanukah* candlestick is being used outdoors at a party.

In Israel today, huge *Chanukah* candlesticks lit by electric lights are placed on the top of large buildings at the time of this festival.

Children play special games. They also enjoy eating doughnuts and potato cakes.

The Feast of Lots

The festival called *Purim* is also known as the Feast of Lots. 'Lots' here means drawing lots – which is like having a raffle. It is a time for having fun. These people are at a street parade in Israel.

This scroll contains the story of ▶ Queen Esther. The story is read out in synagogues during the *Purim* celebrations.

The story of *Purim* goes back to a time long ago in the country of Persia, which is now called Iran.

In those days Persia was ruled by King Ahasuerus. He was married to Queen Esther, who was Jewish. The King had a Prime Minister called Haman who wanted to get rid of all the Jews in Persia. He tricked the King into agreeing to have the Jews killed. Haman then drew lots to decide the day when they should die.

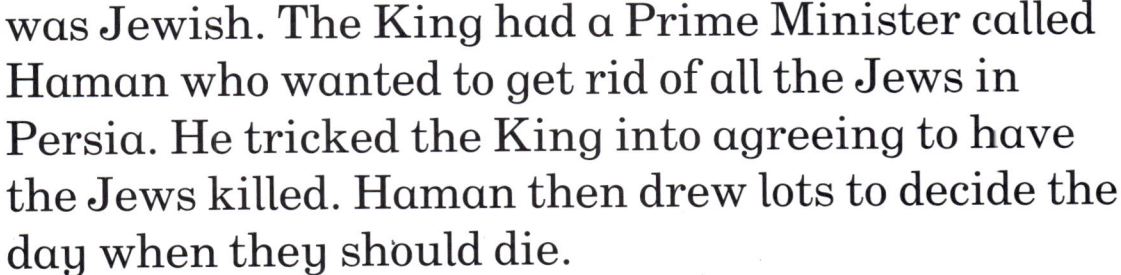

But Queen Esther told the King of Haman's wicked plans. She said that as she was Jewish, she too would have to die. The King was very angry. He had Haman killed, and the Jews were saved. During *Purim*, this story is read out. Whenever the name 'Haman' is mentioned, children make as much noise as possible to drown out his name.

Things to make

The Scroll of Esther
You will need:
a box of greaseproof paper
a flat stick
acrylic paint
strong glue
marker pens

1. Remove the metal cutting edge from the box of greaseproof paper.
2. Cut holes in both ends of the box, big enough to put the stick through.
3. Decorate the outside of the box with paints.
4. Glue the stick to the inside of the cardboard tube.
5. Unroll the greaseproof paper. Use marker pens to draw the story of Esther in the Bible.
6. Use the stick to reroll the scroll.

The noisemaker—to drown out the name of Haman

You will need:
dried beans or uncooked rice
two aluminium foil plates
sticky tape
marker pens

1. Put a handful of dried beans or rice in one of the foil plates.
2. Put the other plate on top and use the sticky tape to join the two plates together.
3. Use the marker pens to draw the face of Haman on the outside of one plate.
4. Now shake the noisemaker and make as much noise as you can!

The Jewish New Year

Jewish New Year is called *Rosh Hashanah*. It is held around September time and lasts for two days. Much of this time is spent in the synagogue.

At New Year a ram's horn is blown to call people to the synagogue. The Hebrew name for this instrument is *Shofar*.

During the services in the synagogue, the Rabbi and the Cantor (who leads the prayers) wear white robes. The colour white is a sign of **purity** and reminds people of the need to make a fresh start at New Year.

The first ten days of the New Year are called the Ten Days of Repentance. It is a solemn time when Jewish people go to the synagogue often. They think about their lives and about how to become kinder and better people.

During the evening meal at New Year, people eat pieces of bread dipped in honey. This is to wish everyone 'a good, sweet year'.

At New Year, Jewish people think of the Creation of the world. They believe God created the world at New Year.

New Year is also known as the Day of Judgement. Jews believe that people are judged by God. If they have behaved well, God will grant them a good life in the year to come.

This is a *Rosh Hashanah* dinner being held in Israel.

These men are studying holy books at the time of *Rosh Hashanah*.

At this time of year Jews ask God to forgive them for all the things they have done wrong in the past. They promise God that they will not make the same mistakes again.

The last day of the Ten Days of Repentance is called the Day of Atonement. It is the most important and holy day in the Jewish **calendar**. The Hebrew name for this day is *Yom Kippur.*

On this day, Jewish people do not work, eat or drink. They spend the day in the synagogue. They listen to readings from the *Torah.*

Passages from the *Torah* are read from scrolls. This Rabbi is showing the scrolls in a synagogue in Tunisia, in North Africa. These scrolls are more than 1,300 years old.

Yom Kippur ends with a service in the synagogue at sunset and with the solemn sound of the ram's horn being blown.

New Year for trees

Jewish people have a special festival for trees. It is held in January or February, when spring is coming and trees are beginning to grow again.

The festival is called *Tu Bishvat*. It lasts for one day.

In hot countries, like Israel, trees are very important. They give shade from the heat. They give fruit for people to eat. Their wood is used for building. So perhaps it is not surprising that trees have their own festival.

Orange trees grow well in Israel. They are often grown on large farms.

Each year, Israeli schoolchildren plant young trees during *Tu Bishvat*. As they plant them they say a special blessing. Jews around the world give money to help plant new trees in Israel.

Israel's Independence Day

Until 1948, Jews did not have their own country. For 2,000 years they had lived in many parts of the world. But on 14 May 1948 a new country was set up for them. This country is called Israel. This day is now known in Israel as Independence Day.

When Israel was first set up, wars broke out between Israel and Arab countries nearby. Many Jewish people died. They are remembered on Remembrance Day, which is the day before Independence Day.

On Independence Day, Jewish people say prayers of thanksgiving. They are happy to celebrate their own new country. All over Israel there are firework displays, music and dancing.

Jerusalem Day

In 1948, when Israel was set up, the city of Jerusalem was divided into two sections. The Israelis were given one section and the Arabs were given the other.

But in 1967 war broke out between Israel and Arab countries nearby. Israel won the war and gained the Arab part of Jerusalem.

This picture shows Israeli soldiers celebrating in Jerusalem in 1967. They are at the Western Wall. This wall had been in the Arab part of the city.

Jewish people now celebrate Jerusalem Day every year. They remember how the Israelis won the whole of Jerusalem in 1967. They hold services and pray to God. This picture shows celebrations at the Western Wall in Jerusalem.

The Western Wall is very special for Jewish people. It is all that is left of their ancient Holy Temple.

The Sabbath

▸ The **Sabbath** begins on Friday evening. A special meal is held when blessings are said over wine and Sabbath bread.

The most important Jewish holiday is held every week. This is the Sabbath, or *Shabbat*, which takes place every Saturday. It is a day of rest. On the Friday evening, the mother of the family lights candles and says a blessing. She also gives money to help the poor.

When the Sabbath candles have been lit, all normal work stops. It is a time to relax and rest.

Adults and children go to the synagogue to pray and listen to sermons. It is a time for special ceremonies too.

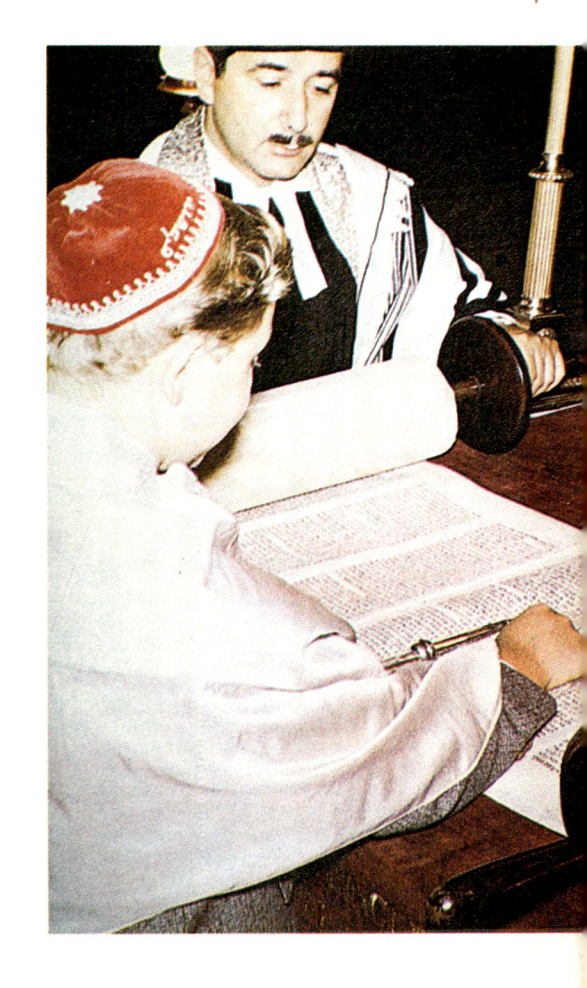

This boy is celebrating his *Bar Mitzvah*. This is a religious ceremony which is held when a boy reaches the age of thirteen. He is then thought of as being grown-up. *Bar Mitzvah* ceremonies are held in the synagogue on the Sabbath. Families and friends gather to celebrate, and then they usually have a party afterwards.

The Jewish calendar

In the Jewish calendar there are usually 12 months each year. In a Jewish leap year, another month is added, making 13 months altogether. Here you can see when the Jewish festivals are held.

Months		Festivals
Tishri	(Sept–Oct)	New Year Day of Atonement Feast of Tabernacles
Cheshvan	(Oct–Nov)	
Kislev	(Nov–Dec)	Festival of Lights
Teveth	(Dec–Jan)	
Shevat	(Jan–Feb)	New Year for trees
Adar	(Feb–Mar)	Feast of Lots
Nisan	(Mar–Apr)	Passover
Ivar	(Apr–May)	Israel's Independence Day
Sivan	(May–June)	Jerusalem Day Feast of Weeks
Tamuz	(June–July)	
Av	(July–Aug)	
Ellul	(Aug–Sept)	

The Hebrew alphabet

Hebrew is the language of Israel. It has its own alphabet. Here are the letters of the Hebrew alphabet. Hebrew words are read *from right to left*.

ה H	ד D	ג G	ב V	בּ B	*א
כ K	י Y	ט T	ח CH	ז Z	ו V
*ע	ס S	*נ/ן N	*מ/ם M	ל L	*כ/ך CH
ש SH	ר R	ק K	*צ/ץ TS	*פ/ף F	פּ P
English has letters called vowels: A,E,I,O and U. In Hebrew these are written as dots underneath or near a letter.				ת T	שׁ S
ֻ / ֻ bUt	ֶ cAke	ֱ nEt	ִ Equal	ֹ pOt	ֹ / ֻ tO

Here are four words written in Hebrew. Beside them you will see how to say them, and what they mean.

1. שָׁלוֹם Shalom – 'hello'.
2. לְהִתְרָאוֹת L'hitraot – 'cheerio'.
3. תּוֹדָה Todah – 'thank you'.
4. בְּבַקָשָׁה B'vakasha – 'please'.

Glossary

Calendar A system for dividing the year into different months.

Commandments The laws that God gave Moses on Mount Sinai. They are the rules that all Jews live by.

Exodus The journey out of Egypt made by Moses and the Jews.

Hebrew The ancient language of the Jews and the official language of Israel today.

Israel The country set up for the Jewish people in 1948.

Israelites The name given to the Jewish people long ago.

Jerusalem The Jewish holy city and the capital of Israel.

Leavened Cooked with yeast to make it light, like bread and some other food.

Miracle An amazing event which people believe was caused by God.

Moses Leader of the Jews. God spoke to him and told him to lead the Jews out of Egypt. He received God's laws on Mount Sinai.

Pharaoh The title given to the kings of Egypt long ago.

Plague A terrible disease or disaster that affects a lot of people.

Purity Being unspoilt or pure.

Rabbi A Jewish religious teacher.

Sabbath The holy day of the week. Jews celebrate this on Saturday.

Scroll A rolled-up piece of paper with writing on it.

Synagogue A Jewish holy building.

Wilderness A wild area of land where no people live.

Books to read

These books will tell you more about the Jewish religion.

A Jewish Family in Britain by Vida Barnett (Religious and Moral Education Press, 1983)

I am a Jew by Clive Lawton (Franklin Watts, 1984)

Jewish World by Sybil Sheridan (Macdonald, 1987)

Judaism by Myer Domnitz (Wayland, 1986)

Light Another Candle: the Story and Meaning of Chanukah by Miriam Chaikin (Houghton Mifflin, 1984)

Passover by Lynne Scholefield (Religious and Moral Education Press, 1982)

Sam's Passover by Lynne Hannigan (A & C Black, 1987)

Acknowledgements

The publisher would like to thank all those who provided pictures on the following pages: Mary Evans Picture Library 4; Sally & Richard Greenhill 5, 9; Sonia Halliday Photographs 10, 34; JNF Education Department 7; Jewish Programme Materials Project 15, 20, 27, 33, 37, 38, 39, 40, 41; The Mansell Collection 6, 8, 24; PHOTRI 31, 35; Picturepoint Ltd. 14, 32, 36; Ronald Sheridan's Photo-Library 16, 17, 21, 25, 42; Rev. Reuben Turner filmstrip: *Judaism—A Way of Life* 30, 43; Malcolm S. Walker artwork 12, 13, 28, 29; ZEFA cover, 11, 18, 19, 22, 23, 26.

Index

Africa 34
Ahasuerus, King 27
Arabs 39, 40

Bar Mitzvah 43

Chanukah 22–5
Charoset 9, 12
Commandments 14, 17

Day of Atonement 34, 44
Day of Judgement 32

Egypt 4–7, 9, 11, 14, 18
Esther, Queen 27
Exodus 7

Feast of Lots 26–9, 44
Feast of Tabernacles 18–21, 44
Feast of Weeks 14–17, 44
Festival of Lights 22–5, 44

Haggadah 11
Haman 27–9
Hebrew 22, 30, 45
Holy Ark 16
Holy Temple 20, 41

Independence Day 38–9, 44
Israel 15, 19, 25, 32, 36, 37, 38–9, 40, 45
Israelites 4

Jerusalem 20, 40–1
Jerusalem Day 40–1, 44

Lots 26–7

Mattathias 24–5
Matzah 8, 9, 13
Moses 6, 7, 14, 15, 17
Mount Sinai 14

New Year 30–33, 44
New Year for trees 36–7, 44

Passover 4–13, 14, 44
Pentecost 14
Purim 26–29

Rabbis 16, 17, 30, 34
Rejoicing of the Law 21
Remembrance Day 39

Sabbath 42–43
Seder 9–11
Synagogue 15–16, 21, 23, 27, 30–31, 34, 43
Syrians 23–5

Talmud 17
Ten Days of Repentance 31, 34
Torah 14–17, 21, 34

Western Wall 20, 40, 41

Yom Kippur 34, 35